focus on the family

Healing
THE HEART

FOCUS ON THE FAMILY

Gospel Light

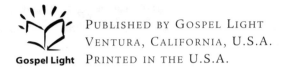

PUBLISHED BY GOSPEL LIGHT
VENTURA, CALIFORNIA, U.S.A.
Gospel Light PRINTED IN THE U.S.A.

Gospel Light is a Christian publisher dedicated to serving the local church. We believe God's vision for Gospel Light is to provide church leaders with biblical, user-friendly materials that will help them evangelize, disciple and minister to children, youth and families.

It is our prayer that this Gospel Light resource will help you discover biblical truth for your own life and help you minister to others. May God richly bless you.

For a free catalog of resources from Gospel Light, please call your Christian supplier or contact us at 1-800-4-GOSPEL *or* www.gospellight.com.

PUBLISHING STAFF

William T. Greig, Chairman · **Dr. Elmer L. Towns,** Senior Consulting Publisher · **Natalie Clark,** Product Line Manager · **Pam Weston,** Managing Editor · **Jessie Minassian,** Editorial Assistant · **Bayard Taylor, M.Div.,** Senior Editor, Biblical and Theological Issues · **Rosanne Moreland,** Cover and Internal Designer · **Jessie Minassian,** Contributing Writer

The Root of All Hurt: The Effects of Sin

Pain can always be traced back to the effects of sin, whether ours, someone else's or simply the sinful state of this decaying world. Understanding the root of hurt is the first step to being mended by the sinless One.

Renewing Your Mind, Part 1: Subtle Deception

Satan knows that the easiest way to successfully deceive us is through our own thoughts. We must understand his schemes if we are to overcome the hold he has on our lives.

Renewing Your Mind, Part 2: Mending Your Thoughts

God never bypasses our minds—He works through them. It is imperative that Christian women fill their minds with what is true, noble, right, pure, lovely, admirable, excellent and praiseworthy as they travel the road toward healing.

Reviving Your Heart: Reconciling Emotions

The emotions we feel are usually direct by-products of the thoughts we think. We must realize that God isn't intimidated by our feelings—He wants to mend them.

contents

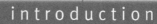

HEALING THE HEART

In this age of personal digital assistants and nanotechnology, it is often said that change is the only constant. We beg to differ. There are numerous constants, many of which we'd rather live without. One such constant can wreak havoc on our lives if we let it: pain. Pain is a part of life, whether we like it or not.

Pain comes in many forms. Sometimes it grows like a slow cancer; other times it cuts instantly, like a sharp knife. Sometimes it stems from our own doing; more often, it comes from circumstances out of our control. Some women handle it gracefully, at least on the outside, while others wonder how they will make it through another hour—let alone the rest of their lives—under the crushing weight of what they've experienced.

God never promised us a life without pain, nor did Jesus experience one while He was on Earth. In the 33 years our Savior lived as one of us, He experienced the same emotions that you and I do. He wept; He laughed; He felt compassion, anger and every emotion in between—yet He did not sin. It's not wrong to feel pain, nor is it a sin to express emotions about our pain, but we don't have to be ruled by our pain. Christ's death and resurrection enable us to experience hope and joy, even amidst overwhelming circumstances.

God wants nothing more than to heal your broken heart. The cause of your pain is irrelevant—God is bigger than anything you have experienced or are experiencing now. No matter where you've been, our prayer is that through the pages of this study, you will begin to let the Master Healer, *Jehovah Rophi*, transform your inmost hurts into conduits of His blessings. That may seem far-fetched now, but don't limit God's power! If He can raise His Son from the dead, He is capable of restoring you, His daughter.

*And this is my prayer: that your love may abound more and more in knowledge
and depth of insight, so that you may be able to discern what is best and may be pure
and blameless until the day of Christ, filled with the fruit of righteousness that
comes through Jesus Christ—to the glory and praise of God.*

PHILIPPIANS 1:9-11

The goal of this series is to help women identify who they are, based on their unique nature and in the light of God's Word. We hope that each woman who is touched by this series will understand her heavenly Father's unfathomable love for her and that her life has a divine purpose and value. This series also has a secondary goal: That as women pursue their relationship with God, they will also understand the importance of building relationships with other women to enrich their own lives and grow personally, as well as help others understand their God-given worth and purpose.

Session Overview

Healing the Heart can be used in a variety of situations, including small-group Bible studies, Sunday School classes or mentoring relationships. An individual can also use this book as an at-home study tool.

Each session contains four main components.

Everyday Woman

This section introduces the topic for the session by giving you a personal glimpse into the life of an ordinary woman—someone you can relate to—and it asks probing questions to help you focus on the theme of the session.

Eternal Wisdom

This is the Bible study portion in which you will read Scripture and answer questions to help discover lasting truths from God's Word.

Enduring Hope

This section provides questions and commentary that encourage you to place your hope in God's plan.

Everyday Life

This section is a time to reflect on ways that the Lord is calling you to change, suggesting steps you can take to get there. It is also a time for the whole group to pray and encourage one another.

Journaling

We encourage you to keep a journal while you are working through this study. A personal journal chronicles your spiritual journey, recording prayers, thoughts and events along the way. Reviewing past journal entries is a faith-building exercise that allows you to see how God has worked in your life—by resolving a situation, changing an attitude, answering your prayers or helping you grow more like Christ.

Leader's Discussion Guide

A leader's discussion guide is included at the end of this book to help leaders encourage participation, lead discussions and develop relationships.

There are additional helps for leading small groups or mentoring relationships in *The Focus on the Family Women's Ministry Guide*.

THE *Root* OF
ALL *Hurt*

THE EFFECTS OF SIN

Consequently, just as the result of one trespass was condemnation for all men,
so also the result of one act of righteousness was justification that brings life for all men.
For just as through the disobedience of the one man the many were made sinners, so also
through the obedience of the one man the many will be made righteous.

ROMANS 5:18-19

EVERYDAY WOMAN

The stillness of the cold night was broken by the shrill cries of a newborn. The mother, exhausted, lay her head down with one final groan. Her husband cut the umbilical cord and tried to clean the baby boy as best he could. The woman, though thankful for her new son, still ached inside as memories of the last time she gave birth flooded her mind. He had been a wonderful son, a ray of sunshine in her life. He had loved the Lord and respected his mother and father. He had helped around the house and cared for the family livestock. He had been the type of son every mother should have. She couldn't imagine what had driven her oldest son to such anger that he would murder his only brother—her dear Abel. Not even this precious newborn baby could ease the intense pain of losing a child. As Adam lay the baby in her arms, she said, "His name will be Seth—appointed—because God has appointed this baby boy to take the place of Abel, my murdered son" (see Genesis 4:25). The moon continued its course across the sky, but Eve couldn't sleep. She thought back to the Garden and the day when all of life changed. *If I had only walked away from that cursed tree*, she thought, *my son would still be alive*. She stroked the hair and kissed the forehead of the sleeping newborn in her arms and began to weep again.[1]

Eve undoubtedly understood the effects of sin more than you or I do. She recognized the pain it caused because for a time she had known life without sin or pain. She must have lived the contrast daily, likely comparing her present pain with the life she and Adam had enjoyed in the beauty and peace of a sinless world. When she found out her son had been murdered in a field, her sorrow must have overwhelmed her, the consequences of the mistake she had made years before must have blinded her with grief.

Because of Eve's disobedience, God told her, "I will greatly multiply your sorrow" (Genesis 3:16, *NKJV*). Eve knew such sorrow well, but the curse didn't end with her. You and I and every woman since Eve have felt the effects of sin—our own and that of others. In fact, every sorrow you have faced or will face in the future is directly related to the sinful state of humankind.

1. Think of the events in your life that have caused you the most pain. How are they linked to sin?

   Anger, Rage

2. Do you think Eve blamed herself for the sorrow she felt when her son died, reasoning that it was her fault that Cain knew evil? If so, did she have reason to blame herself? Why?

   Yes, I think she did. Yes, I think an could see how easy it would have been for her to blame herself, because the choice she made in the Garden affected all of mankind. But, Cain also was responsible for his own dissision.

3. Have you ever blamed yourself for the hurt you feel as a result of another's sin? Explain.

Yes, can't remember a specific time, but know I've done this.

Once we understand that the root of our grief, loss, shame and hurt is sin, we can begin restoration through the promises the sinless One offers us.

ETERNAL WISDOM

The root of pain and sorrow is sin, but it takes many forms. When Adam and Eve sinned, the entire world was affected by the curses God laid on them. Not only were Adam and Eve forced to leave the Garden cursed with endless toil and pain in childbirth (see Genesis 3:16-19), but all creation also underwent a destructive transformation.

The Curse on Creation

God cursed the ground itself because of Adam's sin (see Genesis 3:17-18). No longer would lush vegetation naturally cover the ground. Instead, the land would produce only thorns and thistles, causing mankind to struggle to grow what was needed to sustain life.

4. In Romans 8:18-25, the word translated as creation refers to everything in the physical universe except human beings. List some elements of creation that have been affected by our sin.

The earth, water, vegitation, air

How are these elements of creation "subjected to frustration" (v. 20) and in "bondage to decay" (v. 21)?

Waites for the day when there will be no more death and decay. For freedom.

5. How has the decay of this physical world resulted in sorrow or pain for you or for others you know?

Air quality, water, beauty.

The Curse on Humankind

Through Adam and Eve's disobedience, all men, women and children are subjected to disobedience. Apart from the saving work of Jesus Christ, no one can be completely righteous in God's eyes. A person's heart is inherently "deceitful above all things and beyond cure" (Jeremiah 17:9).

6. According to Romans 1:28-32, what is the state of humankind apart from God?

Hopeless and unreachable, they desire to do what "they want"

7. Share an example of how you have been hurt—directly or indirectly—by the depravity of the world.

It's an "all about me" world. People are inconsiderate, rude, steal, lie, deceive

The Curse of Our Old Nature

Fortunately, God provided a way to redeem humankind from the curse of sin: His Son, Jesus Christ. When we understand that we have sinned and believe that Jesus died on the cross for that sin and was raised from the dead on the third day, we are forgiven from our sins and our relationship with God is restored (see Romans 10:9-10). However, the Bible makes it clear that we do not immediately stop sinning altogether. The curse was overcome by Christ's work on the cross, but we still wrestle with the residual rebelliousness of our sinful natures every day.

8. In what ways have you experienced Paul's struggle with sin as he described it in Romans 7:15-23?

Galatians 5:16-17 makes it clear that even after you have the Spirit of God in you, you will continue to struggle with the desires of your flesh.

9. Look over the following list of sins, as listed in verses 19-21. Check those with which you have struggled in the past. Underline those with which you struggle now.

☒ Sexual immorality
☒ Impurity
☐ Overindulgence, or gluttony
☐ Idolatry (esteeming *anything* more than God) TV
☐ Witchcraft
☐ Hatred or unforgiveness
☐ Discord (quarreling, gossiping, etc.)

☐ Jealousy
☒ Outbursts of anger
☐ Selfish ambition
☐ Dissensions/factions
☐ Envy
☒ Drunkenness
☒ Crude behavior or language

10. How has your own sin resulted in painful consequences with which you have had to live?

How has your sin affected others?

Every time we choose to disobey God, we sin (see James 4:17). There's no excusing or justifying it, but understanding that we will struggle with our flesh until the day we die—or until Christ returns to take us home—can help prevent us from sinking into despair. We have hope in Jesus; He has won the battle against temptation and sin and will help us do the same (see Hebrews 4:14-16).

Satan loves to trap us in a prison of shame. He knows that if he can cause us not only to feel worthless because of our own sin but also to feel responsible for the sins of those around us, we will be harmless to him and his evil agenda.

We don't know if Eve felt responsible for her son Abel's death. But maybe she reasoned that if she hadn't sinned in the first place, Cain wouldn't have murdered Abel. We do know that once Satan has trapped us with temptation and we have succumbed, he loves to accuse us of our sin and fill us with guilt and shame. We can be sure, however, that whether Eve acknowledged it or not, Cain acted of his own free will, giving in to sin and murdering his only brother out of jealousy.

11. Read Genesis 4:6-7. Was Cain warned about the consequences a wrong choice would bring? Please explain.

12. How does Romans 1:18-20 release us from personal responsibility for the sins of others?

God warned Cain about the consequences of his potential actions, yet Cain chose to sin anyway (Genesis 4:8-9). Romans 5:12 reads, "Therefore, just as sin entered the world through one man, and death through sin, and in this way death came to all men, because *all sinned*" (emphasis added). Since the Fall, every man, woman and child sins of their own free will. Eve was not responsible for Cain's actions—Cain disobeyed God's direct command all on his own.

13. In what ways have you blamed yourself for the sin of others?

Even though we live in a fallen world and in bodies corrupted by sin, as Christians we have a hope that transcends the pain sin causes. Not only has God forgiven us for the sins we have committed, but we also have the assurance that someday we will be freed from these inherently sinful bodies, taken out of this decaying world and given new bodies—fashioned after Christ's sinless, resurrected body (see 1 Corinthians 15:20-22,42-45).

14. According to 1 Corinthians 15:20-22,42-45, how does the hope of salvation combat the curse against creation, the curse against humankind, and our struggle with our old sin nature?

We also have another hope as Christians: God's justice. God did not set the world in motion and then take a seat in the top of the bleachers to watch evil run rampant and overcome His children. On the contrary, He is very active in the affairs of men, and He has an insatiable sense of justice.

In Psalm 73, Asaph lamented the fact that evil men seem to prosper. He wondered why he had worked so hard to be pure and innocent when the ungodly were "carefree" and enjoyed an "increase in wealth" (v. 12); but one day as he was worshiping God, he understood their fate (v. 17).

15. According to Psalm 73:17-28, what eventually happens to those who despise God?

Reread verses 23-24. In what ways have you experienced this truth when the sin of others has hurt you? What hope do you find in these verses?

Look again at the events you listed in question 1. Select one to consider in the following format. When you have completed the first one, on a separate sheet of paper do the same with the other hurts you listed.

16. Hurt 1 _____

   Whose sin caused this pain?

   On a scale of 1 to 10, to what extent are you still holding on to this hurt?

1	2	3	4	5	6	7	8	9	10

   I've let go   I haven't let go yet

   What would it take to be healed from this sorrow?

   Sometimes it is difficult to recognize just how hurt we are by an incident, especially if the event occurred quite a while ago. But just as a cut can appear to be healing only to become infected later, it's important that you uncover and clean out these hurts properly. Ignoring your wounds will only allow them to fester longer and become more serious.

   This week, ask the Lord to reveal areas in your heart that need healing. If you ask with a sincere heart expecting an answer, He will make them apparent in time.

Note

1. See Genesis 3—4.

Renewing YOUR MIND

PART ONE: SUBTLE DECEPTION

Be self-controlled and alert. Your enemy the devil prowls around like a roaring lion looking for someone to devour.

1 PETER 5:8

EVERYDAY WOMAN

The university gym was packed for the commencement ceremonies. The weather was unusually hot; a heat wave had hit early and not even the large air conditioners could cool the hundreds of people gathered for graduation. Danica fanned herself with a program, hoping her makeup wouldn't melt before the pictures were taken. She let her eyes scan the back of the gym one more time for her father, reprimanding herself even as she did it. *You know he's not going to come, Danica. It's not like he cared enough to come to your high school graduation or even any of your soccer games. Come on, Dani, he hasn't even acknowledged that you're alive in years! What makes you think you're worth the trip now? He's probably out sunbathing with his girlfriend in California or something.*

The school president finally called the first graduate's name. "Steven Andrews" was heard in monotone over the P.A. system. The gym was filled with applause as each graduate was called to the podium, but Danica didn't hear it. Her mind was replaying a well-rehearsed number that consumed her attention.

No wonder I can't get a date! My own father knows I'm not even worth a plane ticket. Where did I go wrong? I'm probably the reason he left in the first place; that's why Mom doesn't like to talk about it. She saw her mother sitting a few rows from the makeshift stage, her arm around Danica's younger sister. *How could God let this happen to us? If He loved us as much as I thought He did, He wouldn't have let Dad leave.*

The sound of her own name crackling over the P.A. system jolted her back to reality: "Danica Pearson," followed by the customary applause.

As she walked toward the podium and stretched out her hand to receive her hard-earned diploma, she thought, *How could God accept me when my own father doesn't?* As Danica returned to her seat, she mumbled under her breath, "Then I don't need Him either." [1]

Have you ever stepped back and really listened to your own thoughts? Have you been surprised by them and wondered where they were coming from? In his book *Wild at Heart*, John Eldredge wrote, "We are being lied to all the time. Yet we never stop to say, 'Wait a minute . . . who else is speaking here? Where are those ideas, coming from? Where are those *feelings* coming from?'" [2]

1. What was the most recent positive thought you had about yourself?

2. When was the last time you had a negative thought about yourself? Describe that thought.

How often do you have negative thoughts about yourself?

What is the source of such thoughts?

We, like Eve, yield to the same subtle deception with which Satan tempted her. But what form does that deception take? How was Satan able to convince Eve to turn away from the God she knew and loved?

ETERNAL WISDOM

The apostle Peter warned, "Be self-controlled and alert. Your enemy the devil prowls around like a roaring lion looking for someone to devour" (1 Peter 5:8). Satan's influence is not limited to unbelievers. His ultimate goal is to get believers to doubt what God has said, rendering them broken and useless. In order to survive our enemy's attacks, we must be aware of his tactics.

3. According to 2 Corinthians 11:3, how did Satan deceive Eve?

Satan was able to get Eve to turn away from her "sincere and pure devotion" to God by leading her mind astray. He caused her to question what God said and tempted her to live independently of Him.

Just as in a military battle, if you don't understand your enemy's tactics, your enemy will continue to win the battles staged against you. We've already seen Satan's battle plan against Eve—according to 2 Corinthians 11:3, he led her mind astray. The Greek word for "mind" in that verse, *noema*, means "that which thinks, the mind, thoughts or purposes." It is mentioned four other times in the book.[3]

4. Read 2 Corinthians 2:11, which also uses the word "noema." In this verse, it is translated "schemes." What does that tell you about the nature of Satan's strategy against Christians?

Why does Satan choose this tactic? Let's look at it this way: If I were to lie to you outright, you would likely see right through my lie. But if I were to *deceive* you, you wouldn't even know it—especially if that deception was disguised as one of your own thoughts. Most Christian women don't murder, loot or belong to terrorist groups. Satan must take a stealthier approach, knowing that your most susceptible faculty is your mind.

Satan has taken this approach throughout history, from Adam and Eve to you and me. King David was no exception.

Read 1 Chronicles 21:1-7. The Hebrew word for "incited" in verse 1, *cuwth*, means "to allure, instigate or entice."[4] That sounds strangely like Satan's strategy in the Garden of Eden, doesn't it? (See Genesis 3:1-4.) David wanted to number his immense army to satisfy his pride. In essence, he was putting his trust in himself and the strength of Israel, instead of trusting God, who had helped Israel defeat armies many times its size over and over again.

5. Based on what we've seen of Satan's strategy so far, with what specific thoughts do you think he enticed David?

Ananias and Sapphira are another example of Satan's subtle deception. Rather than play on pride, as with David, Satan chose to tempt this couple to lie by evoking their selfishness and greed.

6. Read Acts 5:1-11. According to verse 3, who filled Ananias's heart to lie against the Holy Spirit?

The Greek word for "filled" in this verse, *pleroo*, means "to fill to the full," "to complete," or "to carry into effect."[5] Notice how the same word is used in Acts 13:52, "And the disciples were *filled* with joy and with the Holy Spirit" (emphasis added).

7. Based on the definition of "pleroo," what does it mean to be "filled with joy and with the Holy Spirit?"

8. Practically speaking, how do thoughts correlate with pleroo?

How are your thoughts dependent on who or what is filling you?

9. What sort of thoughts were likely filling the disciples' minds?

10. With what thoughts do you think Satan tempted Sapphira in order to get her to go along with her husband's conspiracy and, ultimately, lie?

ENDURING HOPE

As we've already seen, 2 Corinthians 2:11 warns us to be aware of Satan's schemes, or noema. We've now exposed Satan's strategy, but that doesn't do us any good unless we recognize how he uses mental deception against us individually.

Just as David was tempted by pride, and Ananias and Sapphira by greed and hypocrisy, each of us is particularly susceptible to certain lies. Satan knows our weak points and will pound them relentlessly with accusations, questions and perversions of the truth. Every time we give him an inch, he moves in a foot.

Now it's time to dig a little deeper and identify those areas in which you are most susceptible to Satan's deception. Before you begin this section, take some time to prepare your heart through prayer.

Dear Father, I know that I am Your child and that You want me to live a life free from Satan's deception. Search my mind and reveal any areas of my thought life in which I have allowed Satan to gain a foothold. I want to be filled with joy and with Your Holy Spirit! In Jesus' name I ask these things. Amen.

Below is a chart that will help you identify and document how Satan specifically attacks your noema. Danica's chart has been provided as an example.

DANICA'S CHART

Satan's Deceptive Thought	Plays on My
1. *I'm worthless.*	shame
2. *Guys don't think I'm pretty.*	low self-esteem
3. *It's my fault my father left.*	guilt
4. *If God loved me, He wouldn't have let Dad leave.*	lack of faith in God's sovereignty
5. *God couldn't accept me for who I am.*	low self-esteem
6. *I don't need God.*	pride

Now fill in your own chart. Especially note those thoughts that arise when you think about the hurts you pinpointed in session 1—Satan loves to hit us where we are weakest! Use more paper if needed.

YOUR CHART

Satan's Deceptive Thought	Plays on My
1.	
2.	
3.	
4.	
5.	
6.	

Before you move on, thank God for revealing these areas to you. He may reveal more deceptive thoughts in the days and weeks ahead. When He does, document them in your chart.

EVERYDAY LIFE

Satan's strategy—subtle deception intermingled with our thoughts—calls for serious action on our part. If we are to recognize and combat his lies, we must know the truth of God's word so well that spotting Satan's lies is second nature.

Recognizing Satan's deception is a lot like spotting counterfeit money. When the United States Secret Service trains its recruits to detect monetary fraud, the trainers don't bring in cases of counterfeit money and make the trainees study the imperfections. Instead, the recruits spend hours examining legitimate bills, memorizing each minute detail: the portrait, seals, border, serial numbers and paper quality. Once they are intimately acquainted with the *real* thing, spotting counterfeit money becomes natural. They may not be able to pinpoint the exact flaw in the counterfeit, but they can sense that something just isn't right.[6]

The same is true of your thought life. When you are intimately acquainted with God's truth, any lie that Satan tries to slip into your thoughts will send up red flags. A firm knowledge of the truth is the best defense against your enemy's schemes.

On the left-hand side of the following chart, write down the deceptive thoughts you recorded in the previous section. On the right-hand side, write down Scripture references and the truth that combats Satan's lies.

Satan's Deceptive Thought	God's Truth
Example: *I'm worthless.*	• I am fearfully and wonderfully made (see Psalm 139:14). • Jesus died for me, and I have great worth in Him (see John 3:16). • God values the sparrows enough to take care of them, and I am worth more to Him than many sparrows. He knows everything about me and still accepts me (see Luke 12:6-7).
1.	
2.	
3.	
4.	
5.	
6.	

Dig into God's Word this week. As you read, write those verses that particularly speak against Satan's lies on index cards. Memorize those Scriptures—one at a time—that specifically combat the lies that Satan feeds you. The more time you spend with God, in His Word and in prayer, the more you will be equipped to take a stand against the devil's schemes.

> Put on the full armor of God so that you can take your stand against the devil's schemes. For our struggle is not against flesh and blood, but against the rulers, against the authorities, against the powers of this dark world and against the spiritual forces of evil in the heavenly realms. Therefore put on the full armor of God, so that when the day of evil comes, you may be able to stand your ground, and after you have done everything, to stand (Ephesians 6:11-13).

Notes

1. This story is a fictional account. Any resemblance to actual events or people, living or dead, is purely coincidental.
2. John Eldredge, *Wild at Heart* (Nashville, TN: Thomas Nelson, Inc., 2001), p. 152.
3. "The New Testament Greek Lexicon," *Crosswalk.com*. http://bible.crosswalk.com/Lexicons/Greek (accessed November 3, 2003).
4. "The Old Testament Hebrew Lexicon," *Crosswalk.com*. http://bible.crosswalk.com/Lexicons/Hebrew (accessed November 3, 2003).
5. "The New Testament Greek Lexicon," *Crosswalk.com*. http://bible.crosswalk.com/Lexicons/Greek (accessed November 3, 2003).
6. "Know Your Money: How to Detect Counterfeit Money," *United States Secret Service*. http://www.secret-service.gov/money_detect.shtml (accessed November 1, 2003).

Renewing YOUR MIND

PART TWO: MENDING YOUR THOUGHTS

*Finally, brothers, whatever is true, whatever is noble, whatever is right,
whatever is pure, whatever is lovely, whatever is admirable—if anything is
excellent or praiseworthy—think about such things.*

PHILIPPIANS 4:8

EVERYDAY WOMAN

The pediatrics ward at St. Francis Hospital was beginning to feel like home—
no, it *was* home. Alissa had spent too many nights here to count, watching
silently over her little son, Jensen. Not quite two years old, he had already
undergone half a dozen surgeries. The doctors still couldn't give the family
any answers. Oh, several had tried, but time kept proving even their most log-
ical explanations wrong. Alissa was exhausted. This three-week stay had been
particularly difficult. The doctors had inserted a feeding tube into Jensen's
stomach—no one knew how long he would need it. Now her precious little
boy lay asleep in the hospital crib, the first peace he had known in days.
Alissa reached through the slats in the crib to hold her son's hand, the only
place on his body not connected to a monitor by a tangled mess of cords. The
rhythmic "bleep, bleep, bleep" of the heart monitor caused the fatigue Alissa
had been fighting all day to finally overcome her. She leaned her head
against the cold metal of the crib. Caught in the no-man's-land between

consciousness and sleep, she let her mind wander in a maze of anxiety. *God, why can't you just heal him? He's gone through so much already! Why do you make us walk this never ending road? Lord, I couldn't handle it if he died.* The very thought of losing Jensen made her sick to her stomach. *What if that's what God has planned all along? You're going to take him from me, aren't You, God.* Her shoulders began to shake with silent sobs, as a dark scene played in her mind . . . a field of grass, damp from the rain . . . a funeral procession . . . a small grave-stone . . . her husband in tears . . . pain and grief and darkness . . . *That's what you want for my little boy?* Her thoughts were nearly shouting at God now—trapped and exhausted in the silent sepulcher of her mind.[1]

It's amazing how quickly our thoughts can overrun our better sense, isn't it? How often have you, like Alissa, allowed your imagination to become so real that you felt the feelings of—and maybe even shed tears in—your created world?

1. What was the most recent incident over which you worried and imagined the worse? Did these imaginations come true?

    Do you see any correlation between those destructive thoughts and your physical state (such as being tired, hungry or fatigued)? Please explain.

As we saw in session 2, Satan loves to trap us with subtle deception aimed at our minds, especially when our defenses are down. The first step is recognizing his deception. The second step is mending our thoughts—replacing Satan's lies with God's truth. Let's look a little closer at what that means.

Note: Although Satan is the father of lies, he is not behind every deceptive thought. Our sinful nature often makes us our own worst enemy, and we must take responsibility for our thoughts and actions.

ETERNAL WISDOM

Just as in Alissa's case, wandering, false thoughts replace God's peace with anxiety, fear and hopelessness. The Bible gives us very clear guidelines as to which thoughts and actions will bring about God's peace—a peace that goes way beyond anything we could dream up on our own. As we explore these guidelines, we will camp out in Philippians 4:4-9. These verses are printed here for your convenience. The Greek words we will be examining are in italics—there are a lot, but this passage is particularly powerful when you understand the original meanings *behind* the words.

> ⁴Rejoice [*chairo*] in the Lord always. I will say it again: Rejoice! ⁵Let your gentleness [*epieikes*] be evident to all. The Lord is near. ⁶Do not be anxious [*merimnao*] about anything, but in everything, by prayer and petition, with thanksgiving, present your requests to God. ⁷And the peace of God, which transcends all understanding, will guard your hearts and your minds [*noema*] in Christ Jesus. ⁸Finally, brothers, whatever is true [*alethes*], whatever is noble [*semnos*], whatever is right [*dikaios*], whatever is pure [*hagnos*], whatever is lovely [*prosphiles*], whatever is admirable [*euphemos*]—if anything is excellent [*arête*] or praiseworthy [*epainos*]—think about such things. ⁹Whatever you have learned or received or heard from me, or seen in me—put it into practice. And the God of peace will be with you.

2. According to verse 7, what will guard your inmost being (your heart and your noema)?

The conjunction "and" at the beginning of verse 7 shows that this promise is conditional. It is an "if, then" promise. *If* we choose to follow the condition, *then* God's peace will guard our thoughts. Verses 4 through 6 set up those conditions.

3. What condition is presented in verse 4? Are there any exceptions to this condition? In other words, are there times when we are exempt from rejoicing?

"Chairo," translated as "rejoice" in these verses, means "to be glad; to rejoice exceedingly," but it is often used in the context of expressing greetings to someone; it is *relational* as well as an internal attitude. [2]

4. With the meaning of "chairo" in mind, give an example of rejoicing even in a painful situation.

What condition is given in verse 5?

"Epieikes" means "suitable, gentle, equitable and fair."[3] Titus 3:2 (*NKJV*) further illuminates this word: This verse tells us to "speak evil of no one, to be peaceable, gentle [epieikes], showing all humility to all men." We are called to show these qualities to everyone. As we learned in session 1, the root cause of our hurt and pain is likely someone else's sin. The condition found in Philippians 4:5 does not exclude that person! Rather, we are called to deal fairly and gently with him or her.

5. How have you been temped to speak evil of those who have hurt you?

6. Why do you think Paul mentioned "the Lord is near" right after he told us to show gentleness to all?

7. What is the third condition for peace of mind, as found in verse 6?

"Merimnao" means "to be troubled with cares."[4] We could each testify to womankind's general tendency to be troubled by something as insignificant as a broken fingernail. But generally, our greatest causes of anxiety are those specific hurts or circumstances that we can't control. Paul seems to speak directly to these hurts in verse 6. It's as if he says, "Hey, don't be troubled by anything! It's not going to do you any good! Instead, ask God to heal you and be thankful for all that He has done in your life through your pain."

8. When you satisfy the three conditions we've discussed, verse 7 says that God will "guard" your heart and mind (noema). From what will He guard it?

9. Now that you understand these three conditions for true peace in your heart, write verses 4 through 7 in your own words as they apply to your circumstances right now.

ENDURING HOPE

The amazing thing about the verses we've looked at is that, well, they're *true*! When you choose to rejoice, even in your pain; when you treat everyone— even those who have hurt you—with fairness, gentleness and compassion; and when you pray with a thankful heart instead of letting your imagination run wild, the peace you feel will baffle you. The key here is to *choose* to obey. You probably won't *feel* like you have anything to be thankful for at first, but as you obey, your feelings will follow suit. The same is true of each of the conditions we've discussed.

10. How can a person rejoice (chairo) amidst pain?

Since rejoicing (chairo) is relational as well as internal, who may be able to benefit from a believer's testimony of praise in times of trouble?

11. To whom do you particularly need to show gentleness (epieikes)?

What are two or three practical ways you can be fair, gentle and/or compassionate with this person?

12. Instead of giving into anxiety, what specific requests do you need to present before God?

What can you be thankful for in that situation?

Write to God about the answers you've given for questions 10 through 12. Ask Him to give you the strength to live out these answers and to honor your obedience by lavishing you with His peace.

God never bypasses our mind—He works through it. The peace that He promises is directly related to the right thoughts that we think. It's not enough not to think *wrong* thoughts; we have to replace them with *right* thoughts. (Emptying our minds, as encouraged by many New Age and Eastern religions, only gives the devil more opportunity to fill it with lies.) Philippians 4:8-9 give us practical guidelines for our thoughts. These guidelines—coupled with the Holy Spirit's touch—will mend our thoughts and bring us peace of mind.

The following are the guidelines for our thought life that Paul gives us in verse 8. He tells us that if we think about such things "the God of peace will be with you" (v. 9). After the definition for each Greek word, write one or two thoughts that combat the wrong thoughts and feelings over which you are tempted to become anxious. To help you get started, examples that Alissa might have written appear in italics.

"Whatever is **true** [alethes]"—Definition: true, truthful, loving the truth, speaking the truth[5]

> Example: *No matter how hard the past two years have been, Jensen is still alive.*

◆

"Whatever is **noble** [semnos]"—Definition: venerable, honorable, calling for respect because of character or attainment[6]

> Example: *The doctors and nurses have been so helpful and caring—truly blessings from the Lord.*

◆

"Whatever is **right** [dikaios]"—Definition: righteous, keeping the commands of God, innocent, guiltless[7]

Example: *Forgive me for doubting Your infinite love for my son, Lord. Increase my faith as I trust You.*

◆

"Whatever is **pure** [hagnos]"—Definition: pure from carnality, chaste, modest, immaculate, clean[8]

Example: *Lord, no matter what happens in the future, I will accept Your will and trust You.*

◆

"Whatever is **lovely** [prosphiles]"—Definition: acceptable, pleasing[9]

Example: *I'm so thankful for a husband with whom to go through these times. There are so many women here trying to handle this all on their own.*

◆

"Whatever is **admirable** [euphemos]"—Definition: uttering words of good omen, speaking auspiciously;[10] or kindly patronage and guidance.[11]

Example: *I know that Jensen's life is a testimony of God's grace, and the time we've spent here at the hospital has been full of opportunities to share my hope with others.*

◆

"If anything is **excellent** [arete]"—Definition: a virtuous course of thought, feeling and action; any particular moral excellence, as modesty, purity.[12]

Example: *Jensen has been so brave through all of this!*

◆

"Or **praiseworthy** [epainos]"—Definition: praise, commendation;[13] or officially approving of.[14]

> Example: *Lord, I accept your will for our lives with joy and thanksgiving, and trust that you will not give us anything that we can't handle with You by our side.*

◆

"Think about such things."

Spend this week putting these true thoughts into practice. You'll be surprised how quickly your feelings will follow suit! Allow the Holy Spirit to mend your thoughts and build you up in righteousness. The peace God offers far surpasses the effort it takes!

Notes

1. This story is based on actual events and is used with permission.
2. "The New Testament Greek Lexicon," *Crosswalk.com.* http://bible.crosswalk.com/Lexicons/Greek (accessed November 9, 2003).
3. Ibid.
4. Ibid.
5. Ibid.
6. Ibid.
7. Ibid.
8. Ibid.
9. Ibid.
10. Ibid.
11. *Merriam-Webster's Collegiate Dictionary*, 11th ed., s.v. "auspice."
12. "The New Testament Greek Lexicon," *Crosswalk.com.* http://bible.crosswalk.com/Lexicons/Greek (accessed November 9, 2003).
13. Ibid.
14. *Merriam-Webster's Collegiate Dictionary*, 11th ed., s.v. "commend."

Reviving YOUR HEART

RECONCILING EMOTIONS

Yet this I call to mind and therefore I have hope: Because of
the Lord's great love we are not consumed, for his compassions never fail.
They are new every morning; great is your faithfulness.

LAMENTATIONS 3:21-23

EVERYDAY WOMAN

There he is, watching TV again. What's a girl got to do to get some help around here?
Maggie grabbed the dirty dishes from the coffee table and headed back to the
kitchen. Phil didn't notice her rolling her eyes; after a long day at the office,
he was totally engrossed in *Monday Night Football*. Back in the kitchen, Maggie
scrubbed the pots especially hard. *I suppose he's going to want to get all romantic
too. Ugh! The nerve of that man! Ignoring me all evening and then expecting me to fall
head over heals for him! You'd think that in 25 years of marriage he would've learned
that women just don't work that way!* The scrubbing got even harder as a lump
began to form in her throat. Her internal monologue continued until the
last dish was drying on the rack. *At least when the kids were here I had a distrac-
tion.* She wiped down the counter and headed back to the living room on the
verge of tears.

"Hi, honey," Phil said as she came back in. "Why don't you come sit over
here by me?"

It was the last straw. The tears came freely now, a flood of anger, bitter-ness, rejection and fear flowing down her cheeks. *Oh, don't even try to be all sweet now!* she thought, but no words made it past the lump in her throat and through her pursed lips. Instead, she got up and stormed to the bedroom to let it all out. Bewildered, Phil went back to his football game. He didn't know what to do; he figured that going after her would only make things worse. *It must be a woman thing,* he thought. *She probably misses the kids or something.* He turned over in his hands the small, gift-wrapped box he had hidden under the newspaper, and then slipped it into the coffee table drawer.[1]

Most of us have gone through an experience like Maggie's in which we talk—or rather think—ourselves into an emotional dungeon.

1. How do you suppose Maggie became so cold toward her husband?

   What caused her to progress from calm and collected Maggie to emo-tional-mess Maggie?

2. In what ways do you relate to Maggie's experience?

We've spent the past two sessions learning to recognize destructive thoughts and how to replace them with God's truth. Now let's look at how to reconcile our emotions—how to begin easing the *pain*.

By their very nature, emotions are intricately linked to our thoughts. In the previous sessions, when we learned to replace Satan's lies with the truth, you may have noticed your emotional health already beginning to improve.

The prophet/priest Jeremiah exhibited this principle time and again. He is often called "the weeping prophet" because he expressed his emotions openly. If anyone needed his heart revived, it was Jeremiah. Because of the prophetic words he had brought to the nation of Israel from God—that Israel would fall to the hands of the Babylonians—he was threatened, tried for his life, put in stocks, forced to flee from King Jehoiakim, publicly humiliated by a false prophet and thrown into a pit. Even when Jeremiah's prophecy came true in 586 B.C., it afforded no rest for his weary soul.

His dialogue in Lamentations 3 is a perfect example of how thoughts affect emotions.

3. Read Lamentations 3:1-33 and then describe some of the emotions Jeremiah expressed (or implied) in verses 1-18.

    Who did Jeremiah blame for his woes?

    What did Jeremiah imply about God's character in these verses?

    According to verse 20, what effect did these thoughts have on Jeremiah's emotional state?

4. Paraphrase verse 21, applying it to your own life.

Verse 21 marks a turning point for Jeremiah. After 20 verses of despair, he felt hope! Why the change of heart? The answer lies in his change of *mind*.

5. What emotions did Jeremiah express (or imply) in verses 21-33?

What did Jeremiah imply about God's character in these same verses?

How did Jeremiah's thoughts directly correspond to his emotions?

Even after all that Jeremiah had gone through, there was more to come. A few years later, he was forced to leave his beloved country and flee to Egypt. Our circumstances may not change, but we can still feel joy, peace, hope, and even happiness and contentment midst the storms of life. The key is thinking right thoughts—especially about God's character.

Speaking of God's character, did you know that He can handle anything you want to express? Really. In case you didn't catch that, *God isn't intimidated by your emotions*! "Sure," you're saying, "I know that." But do you *live* like you know it?

6. Do you ever feel embarrassed or ashamed of your emotions or secretly doubt that God accepts you despite them? Explain.

We can't be completely right with God if we aren't real with Him. God created emotions—He knows how they work. That may be part of the reason why He inspired King David to record so many of his ups and downs and all his emotional turmoil. God wants us to know that it's okay to lay our emotions on the table.

In what are known as the imprecatory psalms, David actually cursed evildoers and pled with God to deal justly with the unrighteous. In Psalms 10; 94 and 109, we can practically feel his inner turmoil. In other psalms, David expressed doubt (see Psalm 22:1-2), admitted sin and pled with God to restore his soul (see Psalms 32; 38; 51).

7. Write a short psalm expressing your honest emotions to God. You may want to model it after Lamentations 3 or one of the psalms (wrong thoughts and feelings followed by truth and reconciled emotions). Use another sheet of paper if necessary.

ENDURING HOPE

Have you ever been driving in the middle of nowhere and had your gas light or check-engine light go on? Did you just pass by the next service station, afraid that you would be late or that the problem might be more than you could handle? Like most women, you probably took the opportunity to pull your car over to get some gas or to check under the hood!

Our emotions are like all the little lights on the dashboard of a car. They are *warning* signs, indicating that we might want to take a closer look to discover the problem. In Maggie's case, her emotions were indicative of years of wrong thinking about her marriage and especially about her husband, Phil.

Just like a vehicle's warning system, we have to choose how we will address the problem. There are four ways to deal with our emotions. You can *suppress*, *express*, *obsess* or simply *address* them.

Suppressing emotions is a conscious denial of feelings (as opposed to repressing, which is an unconscious denial of feelings). Women with low self-esteem tend to struggle with suppressing their feelings, telling themselves *I shouldn't feel this way. Something must be wrong with me.* Others might impose a ridiculously high standard on themselves, reasoning *I know better than to feel this way; I'll just have to get over it.*

8. Psalm 32:3 and 39:1-2 are examples of suppressing emotions. What was the result of this suppression?

9. Give an example from your own life of a time when you suppressed your emotions. What was the result?

Expressing our emotions indiscriminately may have more consequences for others than for ourselves. The words we speak or the actions we take in a moment of anger, hurt or frustration can emotionally wound others and permanently damage our relationships with them. The root of responding to emotions this way may stem from growing up in an environment that allowed this type of response. Ironically, women who respond in this way can usually trace their own pain and hurt to that model—and yet they carry on the cycle.

10. Ephesians 4:26-27 and James 1:19-20,26 address the issue of indiscriminate expression of emotions. What are the consequences of this expression, as implied in these verses?

11. Give an example from your own life of a time when you indiscriminately expressed emotions. What were the results of your response?

Obsessing over our emotions means giving too much weight to them. Our feelings—no matter how strong—never justify sin or the contradiction of God's Word.

12. According to Genesis 4:6-7, what was the root of Cain's depression?

What did God say was the prerequisite for Cain's happiness?

We might call someone who overemphasizes her emotions a "drama queen." Everything she does is to draw attention to herself and her needs.

13. Give an example from your own life of a time when you obsessed over your emotions and describe the result.

Addressing our emotions means appraising them honestly, tracing them to their root thought and then deciding if that thought needs to change. As we saw earlier, emotional honesty always begins with God. God's Word and the Holy Spirit will help us wade through the turmoil of emotions to find the root of the problem. First we have to be honest with Him, and then we have to deal with the cause of the emotions. Suppressing our emotions won't help us find healing. Indiscriminately expressing them will only hurt others and cause us to feel remorse and shame. Obsessing over our emotions centers the focus on us rather than on the problem.

14. How does Ephesians 4:25-27 relate to addressing your emotions?

How can you realistically live out this command in your life?

When we put gas in the car or repair the mechanical problem, the little lights on the dashboard turn off. We have fixed the problem, and the warning lights no longer flash. As we address our emotions and take every thought captive, the warning lights will turn on less often. As we honestly identify and address our emotions, the pit stops will become less frequent!

EVERYDAY LIFE

Women are especially prone to emotional traps. The top 10 emotional traps are areas to which Satan knows women are vulnerable, and he is relentless in his desire to ensnare us. We are each susceptible to certain emotional traps more than to others. As you consider each of the emotions in the following list, say a prayer, asking God to search the deepest part of you to reveal any inclination toward that emotion.

Put a check mark beside each emotion with which you struggle. Sample thoughts have been given for clarification.

❑ Jealousy—*She is so beautiful! Why can't I look like her?*
❑ Shame—*He wouldn't love me if he knew the real me.*
❑ Fear—*What if I never find the right man to marry?*
❑ Despair—*How am I supposed to keep going? These circumstances will never change!*
❑ Loneliness—*No one understands what I've been through.*
❑ Insecurity—*I don't think she likes me. Maybe I said something wrong.*
❑ Bitterness—*If my father hadn't been so messed up, I wouldn't be such a wreck.*
❑ Discontentment—*If I could just get out of this town, I know things would be better.*
❑ Doubt—*If God is so good, how could He have let this happen?*

Now read through the list again; then in the space provided write your thoughts that trigger the emotions you checked.

Now, take some time to be honest with God about your emotions. Remember, He already knows what you're feeling—you can't surprise or shock Him! Ask Him to mend your heart as the Holy Spirit empowers you to reconcile your emotions. Pray with the psalmist, "Search me, O God, and know my heart; test me and know my anxious thoughts. See if there is any offensive way in me, and lead me in the way everlasting" (Psalm 139:23-24). Use another sheet of paper if necessary.

Note

1. This story is a fictional account. Any resemblance to actual events or people, living or dead, is purely coincidental.

Redeeming THE WRECKAGE

UNDERSTANDING FORGIVENESS

And what I have forgiven . . . I have forgiven in the sight of Christ for your sake,
in order that Satan might not outwit us. For we are not unaware of his schemes.

2 CORINTHIANS 2:10-11

I firmly believe that a great many prayers are not
answered because we are not willing to forgive someone.

DWIGHT L. MOODY

EVERYDAY WOMAN

December 12. Humph. Happy anniversary, Mariana. Exactly two years ago tonight your world fell apart. What better way to celebrate than to let those memories ruin yet another perfectly good sunset, eh? Ugh, the whole thing just makes me sick. As if it weren't enough that he destroyed me then, he has haunted me every day since. But it seemed so good, so true at first! Sure we were on-again, off-again for a while, but all guys are afraid of commitment at first, right? I'll never forget the night he finally told me he was 100 percent sure this time. I thought I was going to float right out the car window into the starry expanse above. Life was great after that—for a while. I really thought that after 31 years of being single, my patience had finally paid off. Stupid girl. When are you going to learn? Now I can't get the picture out of my mind: my favorite coffee shop, Carlos, and my so-called friend, Susana, holding hands across the table, so starry-eyed they didn't even see me. I thought I was going to vomit. How could he cheat on me with my own friend? That sort of thing happens in tragic novels and cheesy flicks, not in real people's lives! Yet here I am, another victim of naiveté. I'll never be able to forgive him. I mean, I thought I had, but it just kills me every time I think of what he did. I just want the same thing to happen to him so that he knows how that kind of torture feels. Is that so bad to ask, God? It's the least he deserves for forever warping my view of men and destroying my self-esteem, right?[1]

Mariana's story is not uncommon. Perhaps you also have had to deal with instances of rejection and shame. Such wounds cut deep into the heart and are extremely difficult to forgive. Abuse, neglect, embarrassment, untruthfulness—these are all hurts that stem from others' sin, but forgiveness is a necessary part of the healing process.

Forgiveness can be tricky because it is an intangible, and for that reason, we may have difficulty knowing whether we've truly forgiven someone.

1. To which of the following statements do you relate?

    ❑   *I thought I had forgiven that person, but the hurt has never gone away.*
    ❑   *How can I forgive if I never want to see that person's face again?*
    ❑   *This person doesn't deserve forgiveness—what he (or she) did is so unthinkable I don't even want to think about it, let alone forgive.*
    ❑   *I'm not ready to forgive—it still hurts too much.*

2. Is there anyone in your life whom you are unsure if you've completely forgiven or whom you don't feel you can forgive? Please explain.

Our souls can never be completely mended until we let go of the heavy baggage of resentment and replace that weight with the unimaginably light yoke of God's peace (see Matthew 11:29). It may seem impossible now, but once we understand what forgiveness is and—just as important—what it is *not*, we will see that forgiveness is indeed attainable.

Although forgiveness has benefits for those who have wounded us, extending forgiveness is primarily for the sake of our relationship with God and for the benefit of mending our own damaged emotions. We may not *feel* ready to forgive, especially if our wound is fresh, but remember: We don't heal in order to forgive, we forgive in order to heal.

If everything inside of you is screaming *This person doesn't deserve anything, let alone my forgiveness!* think about the negative effects that unforgiveness has had on you, and consider forgiveness for *your own* benefit. Forgiveness is a necessary step, even if it is born out of selfish reasons at first. Why? Because until we forgive those who have wounded us, Satan has a foothold in our minds, a foothold that manifests itself in our emotions.

3. Read 2 Corinthians 2:10-11. The word "schemes" in this passage is the Greek word "noema" (translated "mind" in other verses), which we studied in session 2. What is another way that Satan can attack our minds?

    Who, therefore, benefits from forgiveness? How?

God understands Satan's schemes better than we can, and He has given us the necessary counterattack in His Word. As we have seen in previous sessions, Satan's attacks are largely aimed at our minds. Subsequently, the counterattacks God outlines for us in Scripture largely address the protection of our minds. We've looked at several ways to protect our minds already. Let's look now at one way that specifically pertains to forgiveness.

4. Matthew 18:21-35 describes a parable about forgiveness. Why would God deal so harshly with those who refuse to forgive (v. 35)?

We can't protect our minds if we refuse to forgive others. This passage makes it very clear that we'd be fools not to forgive those who have hurt us because we have been forgiven so much more than justice would deem fair. Remembering the grace God has extended to us is a fundamental way to guard our minds against unforgiveness.

5. What do the following passages teach about forgiveness?

Matthew 6:12-15

Mark 11:25

Galatians 5:14-15

Galatians 6:1-2

Ephesians 4:31-32

If we refuse to obey God's commands to forgive someone who has sinned against us, we jeopardize our relationship with God. Any time we harbor sin in our hearts, we block the lines of communication between us and God. Only admitting our sin and pursuing obedience will rectify our relationship with Him.

But what does forgiveness entail?

6. According to Romans 12:19-21, when someone hurts us, who will seek justice on our behalf? Why shouldn't we seek our own justice?

How have you experienced this in your own life?

The Greek word *echthros*, translated as "enemy" in verse 20, means "hated, odious or hateful."[2]

7. What does this definition tell us about the nature of those we are to forgive?

Does forgiveness necessarily mean that your relationship will be restored with that person? Explain.

8. In what ways can you "feed" or "offer a drink" to someone who has hurt you?

In verse 20, the phrase "heap burning coals on his head" refers to an ancient Egyptian custom. People who wanted to publicly display contrition would walk around town carrying a pan of hot coals on their heads, representing the burning shame and guilt they felt for the offense they committed.[3] When we choose to show kindness to those who have hurt—and may even hate—us, they will be shamed for their animosity toward us. And because such kindness is not the world's way of treating an offender, we will baffle those around us and glorify the One who has forgiven us so much.

In verse 21 we are commanded to "not be overcome by evil, but overcome evil with good." The Greek verb for "overcome," *nikao*, explains just how much weight forgiveness carries. "Nikao" means "to conquer"[4] and is used 15 times in Revelation to describe the Christians who held fast to their faith unto death, and Christ, the ultimate conqueror. Understanding the meaning of "nikao," answer the following questions:

9.   What happens when we refuse to forgive those who have hurt us?

10.   What incredible promises does God offer to those who overcome according to the following verses?

Revelation 2:11

Revelation 2:17

Revelation 2:26

Revelation 3:5

Revelation 3:12

Forgiveness does not mean that we give up hope of ever seeing justice met; it does mean that we give up the right to execute that justice ourselves. It does not necessarily mean that our relationship will be restored; in some

Commentary

cases—such as death or distance—restoration is impossible. It does mean that we should do everything in our power to reconcile that relationship.[5] Forgiveness also means being honest about any sin we may have committed in the relationship—however large or small in comparison—and asking forgiveness for those offenses.

ENDURING HOPE

There is another aspect of forgiveness that brings incredible hope. The most common misconception about forgiveness is that we must forgive and forget. The human mind doesn't work that way! Forgetting may be a by-product of forgiveness, but simply trying to block past offenses from our minds is never a means to forgiveness.

Some might attempt to forgive an offender by vowing never to remember the offense again. Then they feel discouraged and disillusioned when two years—or even two days—down the road, they feel a resurgence of bitterness and a desire to see justice met.

Their misconception follows this reasoning: *God has forgotten my sins, so I must forget the sins others commit against me.* But there is a problem with such reasoning. If God is omniscient—meaning He knows everything—can He ever completely *forget* anything?

11. Read the following Scriptures and note what each says about God's omniscience.

    Psalm 139:1-4

    Isaiah 40:13-14

    Hebrews 4:13

12. According to Psalm 103:10-12, what has God done instead of merely forgetting our sins?

How do Isaiah 43:25 and Jeremiah 31:34 relate to "forgetting our sin"?

What might be the difference between forgetting another's sin and not remembering it? What does your answer tell you about the type of forgiveness you are to extend to others?

Since God knows everything, He certainly knows what sins we committed last week. However, He has chosen to forgive us because Jesus paid the price for our sins on the cross. He *chooses* not to call our sins to mind.

We have already looked at a very famous passage about forgiveness, Matthew 18:21-22, in which Peter asked, "Lord, how many times shall I forgive my brother when he sins against me? Up to seven times?" (v. 21). When Peter asked this question, he thought he was being generous. Some rabbis of the day—citing Amos 1:3,6,9,11,13—taught that since God forgave Israel's enemies only three times, forgiving anyone more than three times was unnecessary—and even presumptuous.[6]

13. According to Matthew 18:22, how did Jesus respond to Peter's question?

Since Jesus' intent was obviously not to count each time we forgive another, what was He trying to teach Peter through His response?

As we explored earlier, even after we have forgiven someone, there will be times when we will want to scream "Haven't I already dealt with this?" The Holy Spirit is powerful enough to wipe out all pain and bitterness once and for all and to heal our wounded souls; yet often He chooses not to and our flesh battles resurgences of bitterness.

When Jesus told Peter to forgive no matter how many times someone sinned against him, perhaps He was thinking of those times when our flesh won't listen to us; when we relive those painful feelings day after day—sometimes hour after hour—for months, and sometimes years. Is it possible that He meant we are to forgive someone 70 times 7 times even *for the same offense*?

14. Have you ever battled resurgences of bitterness and/or pain for an offense you had already forgiven? Explain.

15. Read the parallel account of the Matthew passage in Luke 17:4-5. What was the apostles' response to Jesus' command to forgive numerous times?

When you feel the familiar pangs of hurt from an offense you've already decided to forgive, cry out to the Lord, "Increase my faith!" Remember, as you continue to choose obedience and think about what is true, your emotions will fall in line—maybe not today or even this year, but you *will* experience complete healing through God's incomprehensible power.

EVERYDAY LIFE

By now you should have a pretty good idea about who in your life has caused you the most pain. While keeping those people in mind, as you complete this section think also of those people who have committed smaller trespasses against you.

Before you fill out the questions below, take a few minutes to ask the Lord to open your eyes and your heart.

> *Dear Father, You have forgiven me for so much that I could never repay. I don't want to take Your grace for granted like the wicked servant in Matthew 18. Increase my faith, that I may forgive from the heart. I desire to glorify You by extending to others just a fraction of the grace You have shown me. Show me how to do that, Lord. Amen.*

Answer the following questions for each person you need to forgive. Use another sheet of paper if necessary.

Person's initials _____

What is keeping me from truly forgiving this person?

What words, attitudes or deeds should I apologize for?

What steps can I take toward reconciling the relationship (if possible)?

What prayer can I pray for this person?

How can I show this person kindness?

May God's peace fill your heart and mend your soul as you begin—or continue—this process of redeeming the wreckage that unforgiveness and bitterness has wreaked on your life. Remember, the journey may be long, but you are not alone.

Notes

1. This story is a fictional account. Any resemblance to actual events or people, living or dead, is purely coincidental.
2. "The New Testament Greek Lexicon," *Crosswalk.com*. http://bible.crosswalk.com/Lexicons/Greek (accessed November 30, 2003).
3. John MacArthur, *The MacArthur Study Bible* (Nashville, TN: Word Publishing, 1997), p. 1718.
4. "The New Testament Greek Lexicon," *Crosswalk.com*. http://bible.crosswalk.com/Lexicons/Greek (accessed November 30, 2003).
5. In some cases, it may be unsafe to restore a relationship. You may wish to seek professional counseling to ascertain whether such a restoration would be prudent in your case.
6. John MacArthur, *The MacArthur Study Bible* (Nashville, TN: Word Publishing, 1997), p. 1426.

RESTORE MY HEART, *Jesus*

LETTING GO OF THE PAST

It is for freedom that Christ has set us free. Stand firm, then,
and do not let yourselves be burdened again by a yoke of slavery.

GALATIANS 5:1

Your past is always going to be the way it was. Stop trying to change it.

ANONYMOUS

EVERYDAY WOMAN

"Her name's Jayden, Mom. You're a grandma!"

Carole lifted the little bundle from her daughter's arms. *She's so tiny—so perfect*, she thought. Although Jayden was born a month premature, her features were flawless. As Carole touched her tiny fingernails and watched her body tense and stretch in a huge yawn, tears began to fill the grandmother's eyes. But the tears of joy were mingled with tears of remorse, shame and guilt. Twenty-seven years hadn't erased the painful memories of her decision to abort a baby of her own. *How could you do it, Carole? That life wasn't yours to take.* She kissed Jayden's forehead and pulled her closer to herself.

Closing her eyes, she could almost imagine what it would have felt like to hold that little child. In 1977, she had made some bad decisions. Her father was a minister, and she knew he would lose his job if anyone found out that she was pregnant. She couldn't bear to see her sin cause her family that much grief. At the time, there just didn't seem to be any other alternative. As the years passed, Carole got her life right with the Lord, married a wonderful man and started a family; but shame never wandered far from her side. Nearly every time she saw a little one, her past came back to accuse her of being nothing more than a murderer wearing a mask of spirituality. Now, holding her first grandchild, the pain was fresh. *God, how could I have done it? I can never escape the fact that I took that baby's life. It will haunt me to my grave!*

"She's something else, isn't she?" Carole's husband asked. Carole smiled halfheartedly, suddenly realizing that the others in the room did not know the reason behind her tears.

"Why don't you take her, Dear?" she said, handing the baby to him. The room was closing in on her. "If you'll excuse me," she stammered, and she quietly left the hospital room.[1]

As we read in session 1, our own sin can be the cause of our deepest pain. When we choose to believe in all that Jesus did for us on the cross, He forgives us for *everything* in our past—once and for all. He doesn't, however, erase all recollection of our former life from our memory. He does something even better: He frees us from being a product of our past and offers us new life in Him; however, we must *choose to accept* this restoration and let go of shame, guilt and hurt before we can enjoy our new life in Him.

1. What are some results of the shame of personal sin in today's culture?

2. Describe how you came to accept Jesus and the forgiveness He offers.

How has your life changed since accepting His atonement for your sin?

We can't fix or change our past, but we can see it in light of who we now are in Christ. Let's discover what that means.

ETERNAL WISDOM

White as Snow

Before we can let go of our past, we have to understand the nature of Christ's sacrifice. In the Old Testament, the Israelites were required to offer sacrifices to atone, or pay, for their sins. Each time they slipped up, and on specified occasions, they would have to slay an animal because "the law requires that nearly everything be cleansed with blood, and without the shedding of blood there is no forgiveness" (Hebrews 9:22).

When Jesus died on the cross, He became the sacrifice necessary for our sins—once and for all (see Hebrews 9:24-28). Because of His death and resurrection, we no longer have to make continual sacrifices for our sins. God sees us as He sees His Son: completely spotless.

3. What do the following verses say about the state of your sin?

Psalm 103:10-13

Isaiah 1:18

Romans 6:18,22-23

1 John 1:9

How should these truths affect the way you view yourself?

Free from Your Past

Abortion, sexual sin, bodily abuse (drugs, mutilation, eating disorders, etc.), violence, abuse from others—we may not be able to erase the memory of these sins, but God sets us free from our past in two ways: through forgiving us and by releasing us from the bondage of being a product of our past.

There has been much debate in recent years over whether we are simply products of our environment and our experiences. To some degree, we are undoubtedly affected by those elements; however, because of Christ's sacrifice and the transforming power of the Holy Spirit living inside us, we don't have to be a slave to our past any longer.

Dr. James Dobson said, "To say that adverse conditions 'cause' irresponsible behavior is to remove all responsibility from the shoulders of the individual. . . . We must decide what we will do with inner doubt or outer hardship."[2] The same is true of the shame and guilt we might feel because of our past sin. We can either decide to let it hold us in bondage, or we can choose to see ourselves in light of who we are in Christ and accept the freedom He offers.

4. What sins from your past threaten to hold you captive?

5. What lies does the enemy feed you in an effort to trap you in a cage of shame and guilt?

6. What hope for sinners is found in 2 Corinthians 3:17?

7. What will you decide to do with the inner doubt or outer hardship that you have faced or are now facing?

Prepared for Growth

We can either allow guilt and shame to trap our hearts, or we can replace these debilitating emotions with godly sorrow. The latter can be a catalyst for tremendous growth in our walk with God. The apostle Paul understood this; that's why he didn't regret sending a letter to the Corinthian church to expose their sin. He knew his words would hurt, but he also knew that they needed to hear his rebuke in order to grow.

8. Read 2 Corinthians 7:9-11. According to verse 10, what does the sorrow of the world produce?

What were the results of the Corinthians' godly sorrow (v. 11)?

9. Using a dictionary, explain the words and phrases that describe what godly repentance should produce (v. 11):

Earnestness

Eagerness to clear self

Indignation

Alarm

Longing

Concern

Readiness to see justice done

In what ways should these characteristics manifest themselves in your own life?

In verse 11, Paul wrote, "At every point you have proved yourselves to be innocent in this matter." The Greek word for "innocent," *hagnos*, means "pure" or "clean."[3] He wasn't telling the Corinthian believers that they were innocent of doing wrong but that they had demonstrated the genuineness of their repentance by their resulting purity. They had proven they were sincerely repentant by living the way they should.

Rather than spending energy on shame and grief, channel that energy to a more productive end: Allow your remorse to propel you toward godliness.

Instead of dwelling on the past, allow godly sorrow to produce a zeal in you that will keep you from continuing to make the same mistakes over and over.

ENDURING HOPE

Understanding who you are in Christ is the first step in letting go of the past. Once you understand who you are *now*, you can release yourself from who you were *then*. Take some time to discover your new identity.

10. Next to each of the following verses, describe the characteristic it reveals about who you are in Christ.

    John 1:12

    John 15:15

    Romans 8:1-2

    Romans 8:37-39

    1 Corinthians 3:16

    Ephesians 1:3-8

    Ephesians 2:10

    Philippians 1:6

    Colossians 1:13-14

When Satan accuses you of past sin and tries to trap you in a cage of shame, call these truths to mind. God has forgiven you—don't let the enemy entice you to kick your own backside around the block! Confess your sin, and then forgive yourself as God has forgiven you. Remember the parable of the unforgiving servant in Matthew 18? He mocked his master's grace by refusing to forgive someone when he had been forgiven much. Because of our position in Christ, how much more do we deserve that servant's punishment when we refuse to forgive ourselves?

EVERYDAY LIFE

So far, we've looked at God's forgiveness, the freedom we have from our past, the growth that godly sorrow produces, and who we are in Christ.

11. Based on what you've learned in this session, what would you tell Carole (this week's "Everyday Woman") if you had the opportunity to have coffee with her?

12. What advice would you give someone who is dealing with a situation similar to one you are experiencing or have experienced in the past?

In the space provided, write a letter from God to you, reminding you to let go of your past and embrace your position in Him. You may want to use another sheet of paper so that you can place the letter where you will see it often.

Dear

Love,
God

Notes

1. This story is a fictional account. Any resemblance to actual events or people, living or dead, is purely coincidental.

2. Dr. James Dobson, *Dr. James Dobson's Focus on the Family Bulletin*, vol. 16, no. 9 (Carol Stream, IL: Tyndale House Publishers, 2003), p. 2.

3. "The New Testament Greek Lexicon," *Crosswalk.com*. http://bible.crosswalk.com/Lexicons/Greek (accessed December, 2003).

READY TO *Grow*

THE VALUE OF DISCIPLINE

*He cuts off every branch in me that bears no fruit, while every branch
that does bear fruit he prunes so that it will be even more fruitful.*

JOHN 15:2

*God is not after perfecting me to be a specimen in His show-room; He is
getting me to the place where He can use me. Let Him do what He likes.*

OSWALD CHAMBERS, *MY UTMOST FOR HIS HIGHEST*

EVERYDAY WOMAN

The sanctuary was packed with high school girls, but Charlene wasn't nervous.
It was a talk she had given many times over the past few years, and the words
came easily now. "Girls, there's only one place you're going to find the acceptance and love that you crave in the deepest part of you. Trust me. I know. I
spent years giving my heart away to any guy who showed interest. I wanted so
desperately for someone to cherish me, to find me beautiful and to see the real
me—the me behind the body—that I found myself doing things I swore I'd
never do. As a result, my relationship with God suffered, and I was even emp-
tier than before, caught in a vicious cycle of sin, shame and rejection."

As Charlene told her painful story, she could see in many of the girls' faces
that they, too, had exchanged their emotional and physical purity for a tem-
porary fix of acceptance.

"Girls, take it from me, you won't find what you're looking for in members of the opposite sex. Sure, you may be able to hide your insecurities behind the latest crush for a while, but ultimately, there's only One who can restore your heart. Having your heart broken is a natural consequence of trying to find love and acceptance in the wrong places. Learn your lesson the first time, then cling to your true lover—Jesus Christ."

She was pleading with them now. Charlene knew how dangerous a stubborn heart could be. It took her years to recognize that her broken heart was God's way of disciplining her, His way of teaching her that only He could satisfy her deepest longings for acceptance.

"Don't be stubborn, girls! Accept the Lord's discipline now—it's proof that He loves you more than you could imagine."[1]

Charlene understood the value of the Lord's discipline, but like many of us, it took her years to get to that point. Why are we such stubborn creatures? Like two-year-olds, we can't seem to trust that Daddy knows best, and we constantly reach for every no-no we see. We focus so much on the pain of the spanking that it takes us years (if ever) to grasp the reason behind the spanking.

1. What is one lesson that you had to learn the hard way?

    How has it helped strengthen your faith?

Though it may seem like an oxymoron, God's often painful discipline goes hand in hand with mending your heart and soul. Let's examine the Lord's discipline: what it looks like, why God does it and what it should produce in us.

Types of Discipline

There are two types of discipline on which we will focus: Discipline derived from the natural consequences of our own sin, and the trials or afflictions caused by the sin of others. (**Note:** A third type of discipline is brought about by the effect that human sin has had on the natural world: floods, destructive storms, wild fire, etc. We will not focus on these situations for this discussion.) Let's take a closer look at each of these.

2. List several natural consequences of personal sin (e.g., sexually transmitted diseases, problems with the law, broken relationships).

God can use the natural consequences of our sin to help us grow. Discipline is any "training that corrects, molds, or perfects the mental faculties or moral character".[2] God also disciplines Christians in His own particular way when we sin.

3. List several ways God specifically disciplines Christians because of our sin (e.g., through conviction, feelings of guilt or shame).

Each of these painful results of our sin will lead to growth if we let them. In session 6, we saw one such result of discipline: godly sorrow leading to repentance and ultimately to purity. But what about the trials and afflictions we endure at the hand of another? Does God use them too?

4. According to Psalm 119:67-71, who caused David's affliction?

    What was the result of the affliction David endured?

5. List several ways that God can discipline us through the sin of others (e.g., through persecution and neglect).

Reasons for Discipline

As Christians, we are far from perfect and we need discipline and training, just as our children need those things from us. God uses the trials and sufferings of our lives to educate and equip us. They are evidence of God's great love for us!

6. Read Hebrews 12:1-11. According to verse 6, who does the Lord discipline?

    Of what is His discipline evidence (vv. 7-8)?

What are the differences between your earthly father's discipline and the discipline from the Father of your spirit (vv. 9-10)?

According to verse 10, why does God discipline you?

Who are you to consider when you feel weary and discouraged under the weight of God's discipline (v. 3)?

The Hebrews were being persecuted, but none of them had been exhausted or persecuted to the point of shedding blood or to martyrdom, as Christ had (v. 4). Their pressures, trials and persecution were nothing compared to what Christ endured while He was on Earth.

7. How would you compare the discipline you've endured in your life with the suffering Christ endured (1 being very similar, 10 being very different)?

1   2   3   4   5   6   7   8   9   10

Results of Discipline

8. According to Hebrews 12:11, what does God's fatherly discipline produce?

"Endure hardship as discipline" (v. 7) emphasizes that God can use *any* difficult experience for our benefit, whether it is at the hand of another or as a result of our own sin. Either way, the results are the same. God's discipline produces "a harvest of righteousness" (v. 11).

God is in the fruit-bearing business. He cares about our growth so much that He personally tends the branches—our lives—to ensure the best harvest.

9. Paraphrase John 15:2 in the space provided.

The Greek word *kathairo*, translated "prune" in this verse, also means "to cleanse."[3]

10. Based on what we've learned so far about discipline, how does it correlate with cleansing?

The result of God's pruning, or cleansing, is an abundance of fruit: the fruit of the Spirit (see Galatians 5:22-23), the fruit of righteousness (see Philippians 1:11) and the fruit of the light (see Ephesians 5:8-10).

11. What is the ninefold fruit of the Spirit as listed in Galatians 5:22-23?

12. According to Philippians 1:11, what is the result of the fruit of righteousness?

13. In Ephesians 5:8-10, what composes the fruit of the light?

These fruits are the result of God's discipline. By allowing Him to produce such fruit in us, we remain in Him. But if we refuse to learn from His discipline, we will be cut off from the vine, Jesus (see Matthew 3:10; 7:19; John 15:2). We can't bear fruit on our own; we must remain in the vine (see John 15:4). To remain in the vine (Jesus), we must be willing to be pruned and cared for by the vinedresser (God the Father).

ENDURING HOPE

Perhaps you've felt like Mother Teresa, who said, "I know God will not give me anything I can't handle. I just wish that He didn't trust me so much."[4] Sometimes it seems God pushes us to the breaking point, to the very end of our rope. But until we are pushed to our limit, we never know how much we can grow.

An athlete trains with this principle in mind. Human muscles comprise thousands of fibers. For these fibers to grow, they must be pushed to their very limit—in fact, literally broken (that's why it hurts so much when you push the limits of your body!). When the muscles heal, they become stronger. Your body stuffs the existing fibers with more myofibrils, increasing the muscles' mass.[5]

14. If you never exercise your muscles, what would happen to them?

If you never experience God's discipline, what would happen to your spiritual muscles?

God knows us better than we know ourselves, and He promises never to give us more than we can handle (see 1 Corinthians 10:13). He also promises that He will never leave us (see Matthew 28:20). On the contrary, God draws the closest to us when we recognize that we need Him the most—in the midst of trials. God's hand is never closer than when He is tending the branches.

EVERYDAY LIFE

15. In what ways have you felt the closeness of God's hand in the midst of discipline?

16. In what ways has God disciplined you in the past?

Through your own sin?

Through the sins of others?

17. Do you see any patterns in His discipline (i.e., teaching you the same lesson multiple times)? If so, list the areas below.

In what ways are you resisting God's discipline in those areas?

It's important to consciously recognize the lessons we have learned from God's discipline so that we learn our lesson the first time! Keeping a prayer journal is one way to record for later reflection the lessons you learn and to remind yourself not to go down that road again. It also serves as a perpetual reminder to thank God for the growth His discipline has produced in your life.

In the space provided or in your prayer journal, spend some time thanking God for the discipline you recorded in question 17. Tell Him exactly what you learned from the experiences, and thank Him for using the fruits they produced, or will produce, for His glory. If you recognize areas in your life where you are resisting His discipline, repent them now, and ask God to change your heart.

Dear Lord,

Amen

Notes

1. This story is a fictional account. Any resemblance to actual events or people, living or dead, is purely coincidental.
2. *Merriam-Webster's Collegiate Dictionary*, 11th ed., s.v. "discipline."
3. "The New Testament Greek Lexicon," *Crosswalk.com*. http://bible.crosswalk.com/Lexicons/Greek (accessed December 8, 2003).
4. Mother Teresa, quoted at "Famous Quotes," *Brainy Quote*. http://www.brainyquote.com/quotes/quotes/m/mothertere101983.html (accessed November 14, 2003).
5. Josh Landau, "Olympic Gold: The Ukraine Experience," *University of North Carolina School of Medicine*, August 30, 2001. http://www.med.unc.edu/medal/olympicgold/training.htm (accessed December 8, 2003).

A REASON TO
Dance

THE CHARACTER OF A HEALED HEART

You turned my wailing into dancing; you removed my sackcloth and
clothed me with joy, that my heart may sing to you and not be silent.
O Lord my God, I will give you thanks forever.

PSALM 30:11-12

EVERYDAY WOMAN

Reina's breath came in billows of foggy moisture in the cold morning air. Even in late May, Yosemite National Park was still quite chilly, especially so early in the morning. Dawn's first rays coated the peaks with golden warmth, melting slowly toward the valley floor. Reina had decided to get some fresh air before the rest of the family got up. Each May she and her husband brought the kids to Yosemite for a family vacation, but she had never enjoyed it much; she had trouble enjoying anything. But this year was different. As she walked past Yosemite Falls, she couldn't contain her joy any longer. *Lord, this is beautiful! I can't believe that in the 11 years we've been coming here, I've never noticed just how blatantly you have displayed yourself all over this place!*

Reina had been noticing a lot of other things lately too. The hope and joy she experienced daily baffled her. For the first time in years, she truly felt free from the pain that had consumed her most of her life. Her eyes glimpsed a patch of goldenrods sprinkled with blue larkspur and white daisies by the side of the trail. She drew closer. *That's me, Lord! After a long, hard winter, your warmth has drawn me from the cold, familiar earth and has caused me to blossom in splendid colors. Just as with these flowers, I pray that all who pass by me and notice the miracle you have done in my life will glorify You, knowing that they too can experience the joy of a new beginning.*[1]

Depth of experience is governed by contrasts. Those who have known hunger understand the delight of a full stomach. Those who live in Washington are giddy with one glimpse of the sun. Residents of Montana savor every moment of a winter vacation in Florida. In the same way, those who have been delivered from much feel freedom to a degree others can't imagine. To those who have been broken, a mended soul is a reason to dance in the streets! We are able to rejoice in ways that those who have never felt pain can't begin to comprehend.

1. List some of the evidences that you have seen of God's presence in your life.

ETERNAL WISDOM

At this point, you may or may not feel completely restored, and that's okay. Healing is a process, and it takes longer for some people than for others—especially when the wounds are deep. As you continue to apply the principles we've studied, God will faithfully complete the work He has begun in your heart (see Philippians 1:6).

Even if you feel completely restored now, there may be seasons in your life down the road when you will revisit some of the pain you've overcome during this study. Don't fear those times. Simply start at the beginning: Take every thought captive, be aware of Satan's schemes, forgive again if necessary, and consider those times as yet another way the Lord has chosen to prune you to make you stronger, to allow you to bear more fruit.

With that said, let's look at some characteristics of a mended soul, a healed heart.

Hope

In the New Testament, the Greek word translated as "hope" is *elpis*, which means "expectation of good." The verb *elpo* means "to anticipate, usually with pleasure." In the Christian sense, "elpis" means "joyful and confident expectation of eternal salvation."[2] Of course, every Christian—whether emotionally broken or not—is assured of eternity with God. But the *hope* of salvation, the anticipation of it, belongs only to those whose focus is off their own pain and intently on Christ. The anticipation of heaven should fill your heart with pleasure!

2. Read 1 Peter 1:3-7. According to verse 3, what has God given us through Jesus' resurrection?

Although "for a little while you may have had to suffer grief in all kinds of trials" (v. 6), in what should you "greatly rejoice"?

We've already looked at the definition of "elpis" in verse 3. Let's look now at the term translated as "living" in verse 3. The Greek word *zao* when used as an adjective means "active, powerful and efficacious."[3]

3. How could the hope of spending eternity with God be active, powerful and effective in your own life?

4. What aspect of our hope is described in 1 Peter 1:4?

5. According to verse 5, what hope do we have while on Earth?

6. Consider verses 6 and 7. What specific trials have you faced, and what was the ultimate purpose of the suffering you endured?

Freedom

Another characteristic of a healed heart is freedom—freedom from the top 10 emotional traps discussed in session 4, freedom from Satan's lies and freedom from the cycle of bondage.

7. According to Luke 4:18-19, what did Jesus come to do?

8. Once you have received Christ as your Savior, the Holy Spirit dwells within you. According to 2 Corinthians 3:17, what does His presence bring with His indwelling?

9. According to Galatians 5:1, the freedom Christ gives is absolute. Who is the only one who can put the yoke of slavery back on you?

Joy

A healed heart fills the body with life. Though circumstances may not change, once your heart is renewed, you can sing with David, "You turned my wailing into dancing . . . and clothed me with joy" (Psalm 30:11).

10. Read Psalm 30 and select a verse that particularly touches or applies to you. Write that verse in the space provided.

11. In verses 8 through 10, how did David imply that God would benefit from sparing him?

12. According to verse 12, how did God's mercy on David ultimately glorify Himself?

In what ways will God be glorified through His mercy to you?

The presence of joy in your life is evidence that your thoughts are in line with God's truth. Just thinking about the hope you have in Christ should be enough to start your feet dancing, not to mention the freedom He has given you from Satan's lies and your own sin! Though God never intended for the circumstances in your life to be fairy-tale perfect, He does intend for you to find joy, freedom and hope in Him.

ENDURING HOPE

In session 1, we learned that the root of all the hurt and pain we feel in life is someone's sin—ours or someone else's. Because of Adam and Eve's sin, creation is cursed, humankind is cursed, and even as Christians we struggle with our inherently sinful flesh. But in heaven—the source of the hope which we just discussed—that curse will be lifted.

13. Since there will be no curse of sin in heaven, what does that imply about the presence of pain there?

14. According to Revelation 21:3-5, what is the "old order" that will pass away (v. 4)?

By necessity, what things will pass away with the old order?

This passage is amazing. We could read it 30 times, and each time we would catch just another glimpse of one minuscule reality of heaven. Before you move on to the next section, take a few minutes just to bask in the hope you have of eternity *without sin*. Let it become real to you.

EVERYDAY LIFE

One of the many amazing things about the Body of Christ is the way our experiences can benefit others. Proverbs 27:17 states, "As iron sharpens iron, so one man sharpens another." Whether or not you are completely through the healing process, begin sharing with others what God has been doing in your life. Allow other members of your spiritual family to benefit from your experiences. Perhaps they have struggled, or are currently struggling, with similar circumstances; regardless of whether others can relate to your circumstances, they can glorify God in heaven for all He is doing in your life.

Don't let your testimony stop with other believers! Even if they think you're crazy at first, share your soul-mending experience with non-Christian friends, especially those who have known you since before the healing process began. You are a living, breathing witness of God's power to change hearts. Let Him use you!

You probably won't understand the full scope of all that God has done at first, and that's okay. The words may come haltingly, you may be embarrassed, or you may not have any clue what you're going to say—that's okay too. Just *share*. If you don't feel comfortable talking to others about it at first, begin by writing it out. If you keep a journal, it can act as the place where you find ways to articulate the inexpressible.

Oswald Chambers put it this way:

> Struggle to re-express some truth of God to yourself, and God will use that expression to someone else. . . . Go through the winepress of God where the grapes are crushed. You must struggle to get expression experimentally; then there will come a time when that expression will become the very wine of strengthening to someone else. . . . Try to state to yourself what you feel implicitly to be God's truth, and you give God a chance to pass it on to someone else through you.[4]

Whether on paper or through words, as you share what God has done in your life, the process He has taken you through will clarify, you will begin to see aspects of your journey that you didn't notice before; and in the end, others will benefit from your growth.

Take some time to document your journey, using the following page, a separate journal or by talking with a friend or loved one. Take enough time to really contemplate the steps you've taken toward healing. Talk to God as you recap your journey, thanking Him for healing your heart and rejoicing that your "present sufferings are not worth comparing with the glory that will be revealed in [you]" (Romans 8:18). Then allow Him to use your experiences for His glory.

Notes

1. This story is a fictional account. Any resemblance to actual events or people, living or dead, is purely coincidental.
2. "The New Testament Greek Lexicon," *Crosswalk.com.* http://bible.crosswalk.com/Lexicons/Greek (accessed December 15, 2003).
3. Ibid.
4. Oswald Chambers, *My Utmost for His Highest* (Grand Rapids, MI: Discovery House Publishers, 1963), p. 350.

Healing
THE HEART

General Guidelines

1. Your role as a facilitator is to get women talking and discussing areas in their lives that are hindering them in their spiritual growth and personal identity.
2. Be mindful of the time. There are four sections in each study. Don't spend too much time on one section unless it is obvious that God is working in people's lives at a particular moment.
3. Emphasize that the group meeting is a time to encourage and share with one another. Stress the importance of confidentiality—what is shared stays within the group.
4. Fellowship time is very important in building small-group relationships. Providing beverages and light refreshments either before or after each session will encourage a time of informal fellowship.
5. Encourage journaling as it helps women apply what they are learning and stay focused during personal devotional time.
6. Most women lead very busy lives; respect group members by beginning and ending meetings on time.
7. Always begin and end the meetings with prayer. If your group is small, have the whole group pray together. If it is larger than 10 members, form groups of 2 to 4 to share and pray for one another.

   One suggestion is to assign prayer partners each week. Encourage each group member to complete a Prayer Request Form as she arrives. Members can select a prayer request before leaving the meeting and pray for that person during the week. Or two women can trade prayer requests and then pray for each other at the end of the meeting and throughout the week. Encourage them to call their prayer partner at least once during the week.

8. Another highly valuable activity is to encourage the women to memorize the key verse each week.

9. Be prepared. Pray for your preparation and for the group members during the week. Don't let one person dominate the discussion. Ask God to help you draw out the quiet ones without putting them on the spot.

10. Enlist the help of other group members to provide refreshments, to greet the women, to lead a discussion group or to call absentees to encourage them, etc. Whatever you can do to involve the women will help bring them back each week.

11. Spend time each meeting worshiping God. This can be done either at the beginning or the end of the meeting.

How to Use the Material

Suggestions for Group Study

There are many ways that this study can be used in a group situation. The most common way is a small-group Bible study format. However, it can also be used in a women's Sunday School class. However you choose to use it, here are some general guidelines to follow for group study:

- Keep the group small—8 to 12 participants is probably the maximum for effective ministry, relationship building and discussion. If you have a larger group, form smaller groups for the discussion time, selecting a facilitator for each group.
- Ask the women to commit to regular attendance for the eight weeks of the study. Regular attendance is a key to building relationships and trust in a group.
- Whatever is discussed in the group meetings is to be held in strictest confidence among group members only.

Suggestions for Mentoring Relationships

This study also lends itself for use in relationships in which one woman mentors another woman. Women in particular are admonished in Scripture to train other women (see Titus 2:3-5).

- A mentoring relationship could be arranged through a system set up by a church or women's ministry.
- A less formal way to start a mentoring relationship is for a younger woman or new believer to take the initiative and approach an older or more spiritually mature woman who exemplifies the Christlike life and ask to meet with her on a regular basis. Or the reverse might be a more mature woman who approaches a younger woman or new believer to begin a mentoring relationship.
- When asked to mentor, someone might shy away, thinking that she could never do that because her own walk with the Lord is less than perfect. But just as we are commanded to disciple new believers, we must learn to disciple others to strengthen their walk. The Lord has promised to be "with you always" (Matthew 28:20).
- When you agree to mentor another woman, be prepared to learn as much or more than the woman you will mentor. You will both be blessed by the mentoring relationship built on the relationship you have together in the Lord.

There are additional helps for mentoring relationships or leading small groups in *The Focus on the Family Women's Ministry Guide*.

SESSION ONE—
THE ROOT OF ALL HURT:
The Effects of Sin

Before the Meeting

The following preparations should be made before each meeting:

1. Gather materials for making name tags (if women do not already know each other and/or if you do not already know everyone's name). Also

gather extra pens or pencils and Bibles to loan to anyone who may need them.

2. Make photocopies of the Prayer Request Form (available in *The Focus on the Family Women's Ministry Guide*), or provide 3x5-inch index cards for recording requests.

3. Read through your own answers, and mark the questions that you especially want to have the group discuss.

In preparations specific to *this* meeting:

4. Collect newspapers and magazines, scissors, poster board and glue or transparent tape for the ice-breaker activity.

Ice Breakers

1. Distribute Prayer Request Forms, or index cards, and ask each woman to at least write down her name, even if she doesn't have a specific prayer request. This way, someone can pray for her during the upcoming week. This can be done each week. Just because we don't have a specific prayer request doesn't mean we don't need prayer!

2. Introduce yourself and share something unique about yourself. Have each woman in the group do likewise.

3. On pieces of poster board, have the group make collages made of newspaper and magazine article headlines that have to do with the effects of sin—murders, abuse, theft, divorce, adultery, death, etc.—in the world. This will be used later in the meeting.

Discussion

1. **Everyday Woman**—Discuss what it must have been like for Eve to have known both a life without sin and a life wrought with the effects of her own sin. Invite volunteers to share their answers to questions 1 through 3, being sensitive to those who may not feel comfortable enough to share.

2. **Eternal Wisdom**—Discuss questions 4 through 8, using discretion with regard to personal questions such as 9 and 10.

   Using the collages they made earlier, categorize each (or a handful, depending on the time) of the article headlines under one of the three aspects of the curse: the curse on creation, the curse on humankind or the curse of our old nature. Summarize or explain each aspect of the curse if necessary.

3. **Enduring Hope**—Discuss questions 11 through 14 as a group. Have someone read Psalm 73:18-28, and then discuss question 15.

4. **Everyday Life**—Divide women into groups of three or four women each. Encourage each woman to share with her group the hurts she recorded in this section and how those hurts are affecting her today. Be sensitive to those who may fear being vulnerable at such an early stage in the study, but encourage them to be as open as possible.

5. **Close in Prayer**—An important part of any small-group relationship is the time spent in prayer for one another. This may be done in a number of ways. Here are two suggestions:

   a. Have each woman write out her specific prayer requests on the Prayer Request Forms, or index cards. These requests may then be shared with the whole group or traded with another woman as a prayer partner for the week. If requests are shared with the whole group, pray as a group before adjourning the meeting; if requests are traded, allow time for the prayer partners to pray together.

   b. Gather the whole group together and lead them in guided prayer.

6. **Encourage Scripture Memory**—One very effective way to heal the heart is to memorize God's Word. Encourage the women to memorize the week's key verse or a verse from the lesson that was especially helpful for them. Provide an opportunity at each meeting for the women to recite their memory verses. *The Focus on the Family Women's Ministry Guide* contains additional information on encouraging Scripture memorization.

After the Meeting

1. **Evaluate**—Spend time evaluating the meeting's effectiveness (see *The Focus on the Family Women's Ministry Guide*, "Reproducible Forms" section).

2. **Encourage**—During the week, try to contact each woman (through phone calls, notes of encouragement, e-mails or instant messages) and welcome her to the study. Make yourself available to answer any questions or concerns the women may have and generally get to know them. If you have a large group, enlist the aid of other women in the group to contact others.

3. **Equip**—Complete the Bible study.
4. **Pray**—Prayerfully prepare for the next meeting, praying for each woman and your own preparation. Discuss with the Lord any apprehension, excitement or anything else that is on your mind regarding the Bible study material or the group members. If you feel inadequate or unprepared, ask for strength and insight. If you feel tired or burdened, ask for God's light yoke. Whatever it is you need, ask God for it. He will provide!

SESSION TWO—
RENEWING YOUR MIND
Part One: Subtle Deception

Before the Meeting

1. Make the usual preparations as listed on pages 86-87.
2. Using brightly colored felt-tip pens, copy "Danica's Chart" (or your own chart, if you are willing) on a piece of poster board in preparation for discussion.
3. Make the necessary preparations for the ice-breaker activity.

Ice Breakers

1. As each woman enters, make sure she makes a name tag and picks up a Prayer Request Form, or index card. Encourage the women to at least write their names on their form, or index card, whether or not they have prayer requests.
2. Invite volunteers to recite the memory verse, or recite it as a group.
3. Understanding the original context and meaning of the passages we study is important. Spend some time explaining why using Greek and Hebrew lexicons, as well as other study materials, can help us understand the Bible. Have at least one lexicon available for the women to browse through—you may be able to check out one from your church's library or borrow one from your pastor—and give a short demonstration of how to use it (or invite a pastor or other guest to demonstrate its use).
4. Have each woman share her answer to question 1.

Discussion

1. **Everyday Woman**—Ask the women to share their thoughts on the opening story. Ask if any of them have had feelings similar to Danica's. Discuss the last part of question 2 about the source of negative thoughts.

2. **Eternal Wisdom**—Form groups of two or three women each to discuss questions 3 through 10.

3. **Enduring Hope**—Bring the entire group back together. Display "Danica's Chart" (or your own chart) that you prepared beforehand. After discussing each deceptive thought, encourage the women to share some of the thoughts from their own charts.

4. **Everyday Life**—As each woman shares the deceptive thoughts with which she struggles, invite group members to encourage her with God's truth on the subject.

5. **Close in Prayer**—Have the women stand in a circle and pray brief prayers that revolve around the truths that were shared in the previous section. As the women leave, have them select someone else's Prayer Request Form, or index card, so that they can pray for that person during the coming week. Encourage them to touch base with their prayer partners during the week.

After the Meeting

1. **Evaluate.**
2. **Encourage.**
3. **Equip.**
4. **Pray.**

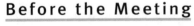

SESSION THREE—
RENEWING YOUR MIND
Part Two: Mending Your Thoughts

Before the Meeting

1. Make the usual preparations as listed on pages 86-87.

Ice Breakers

1. Distribute the Prayer Request Forms, or index cards, and then remind the women to write down their names, even if they don't have specific requests this week.
2. Invite volunteers to recite the memory verse, or recite it as a group.
3. Invite volunteers to share how they applied what they learned in last week's session.

Discussion

1. **Everyday Woman**—Briefly discuss how easy it is for us as women to let our imaginations run wild. Invite volunteers to share serious or humorous personal examples on the subject.
2. **Eternal Wisdom**—Invite a volunteer to read Philippians 4:4-9 aloud. Discuss questions 2 through 8 and then have the women list the three conditions for peace of mind (questions 2, 4 and 7). Invite volunteers to share their answers to question 9.
3. **Enduring Hope**—Have the women form pairs to discuss questions 10 through 12.
4. **Everyday Life**—Invite volunteers to share their answers to one of the eight aspects of right thoughts. They may share more than once if necessary.
5. **Close in Prayer**—Spend some time as a group asking the Holy Spirit to mend your thoughts and build each of you up in righteousness. Invite the women to select a Prayer Request Form, or index card, for the week and encourage them to contact their prayer partner at least once during the week.

After the Meeting

1. **Evaluate.**
2. **Encourage.**
3. **Equip.**
4. **Pray.**

REVIVING YOUR HEART:
Reconciling Emotions

Before the Meeting

1. Make the usual preparations as listed on pages 86-87.
2. Make the necessary preparations for the ice-breaker activity.
3. Gather a sheet of poster board and a felt tip marker, or a white board and dry-erase markers.

Ice Breakers

1. Distribute the Prayer Request Forms, or index cards, and then remind the women to write down their names, even if they don't have specific requests this week.
2. Invite volunteers to recite the memory verse, or recite it as a group.
3. Play a game of Guess That Emotion. Form two teams. The rules are similar to Pictionary, but instead of drawing pictures, each team chooses someone to act out an emotion without using any words. Have small prizes, such as tea light candles, bookmarks or candy bars, for the winning team.

Discussion

1. **Everyday Woman**—Discuss question 1 and the mental progression that can take someone from being calm and collected to an emotional mess.
2. **Eternal Wisdom**—Briefly review how thoughts are linked to emotions. Allow the women to share their thoughts on the subject. Read Lamentations 3:21 aloud, and then discuss questions 3 through 6.
3. **Enduring Hope**—Discuss the questions dealing with the four models of handling emotions: suppressing, expressing, obsessing and addressing. Ask each woman to share in which way she tends to deal with her emotions. As a group, brainstorm healthy ways to address emotions. Write the suggestions on the poster board or white board.

4. **Everyday Life**—Form groups of two or three women each. Have the women share with their group which of the top 10 emotional traps they checked. Have the small groups brainstorm ways to combat the thoughts associated with those emotional traps.

5. **Close in Prayer**—While still in small groups, have the women pray for each other, asking God to reconcile their emotions as they seek to think correctly. Invite the women to select a Prayer Request Form, or index card, for the week, and encourage them to contact their prayer partner at least once during the week.

After the Meeting

1. **Evaluate.**
2. **Encourage.**
3. **Equip.**
4. **Pray.**

SESSION FIVE—
REDEEMING THE WRECKAGE:
Understanding Forgiveness

Before the Meeting

1. Make the usual preparations as listed on pages 86-87.
2. Make the necessary preparations for the ice-breaker activity.

Ice Breakers

1. Distribute the Prayer Request Forms, or index cards, and then remind the women to write down their names, even if they don't have specific requests this week.
2. Invite volunteers to recite the memory verse, or recite it as a group.
3. Provide brightly colored felt-tip markers, and invite the women to write on a poster board things for which they have been forgiven. Encourage

the women to make their contributions creative and colorful—a symbol of the joy that comes with being forgiven of much.

Discussion

1. **Everyday Woman**—Discuss the statements from question 1 that keep some people from forgiveness. Invite the women to share the personal reservations that have kept them from forgiving.
2. **Eternal Wisdom**—Discuss questions 3 through 10 with the entire group.
3. **Enduring Hope**—Discuss the concept of forgiving 70 times 7 times; then invite volunteers to share their answers to questions 11 and 12. Finish this section with prayer, asking God to increase each woman's faith to a level where she is able to forgive as many times as it takes!
4. **Everyday Life**—Encourage the group members to follow through with their answers to this section. Invite volunteers to share (even if vaguely) how they plan to apologize to, pray for or show kindness to one person they need to forgive so that the group can hold them accountable. If appropriate, invite the women to partner with someone in the group who will keep them accountable to complete the forgiveness process.
5. **Close in Prayer**—In pairs, have the women pray for each other's specific requests. As the women leave, have them select someone else's Prayer Request Form, or index card, so that they can pray for that person during the coming week.

After the Meeting

1. **Evaluate.**
2. **Encourage.**
3. **Equip.**
4. **Pray.**

RESTORE MY HEART, JESUS:
Letting Go of the Past

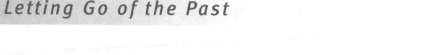

Before the Meeting

1. Make the usual preparations as listed on pages 86-87.
2. Make the necessary preparations for the ice-breaker activity you choose.
3. Gather a poster board and a felt-tip marker.

Ice Breakers

1. Distribute the Prayer Request Forms, or index cards, and then remind the women to write down their names, even if they don't have specific requests this week.
2. Invite volunteers to recite the memory verse, or recite it as a group.
3. **Option 1:** Have each woman share a favorite childhood memory. Discuss the effects that memories have on who we are today.
4. **Option 2:** As you call group members during the week, ask one or two women if they would be willing to share during the meeting their answer to question 2, describing their stories of accepting forgiveness from Jesus and how that has changed their lives.

Discussion

1. **Everyday Woman**—Invite the women to share their answers to question 1. Write the responses on the poster board.
2. **Eternal Wisdom**—Invite volunteers to read aloud the verses listed in question 3 and then share their answers. Discuss questions 4 through 9 with the entire group.
3. **Enduring Hope**—Divide the nine verses in question 10 among smaller groups of three or four women each, and give the groups a few minutes to share their answers among themselves.
4. **Everyday Life**—Discuss questions 11 and 12, being mindful of the time.

5. **Close in Prayer**—Form a circle and pray brief prayers that express our identity in Christ. As the women leave, have them select someone else's Prayer Request Form, or index card, so that they can pray for that person during the coming week.

After the Meeting

1. **Evaluate.**
2. **Encourage.**
3. **Equip.**
4. **Pray.**

SESSION SEVEN—
READY TO GROW:
The Value of Discipline

Before the Meeting

1. Make the usual preparations as listed on pages 86-87.
2. Make the necessary preparations for the ice-breaker activity you choose.

Ice Breakers

1. Distribute the Prayer Request Forms, or index cards, and then remind the women to write down their names, even if they don't have specific requests this week.
2. Invite volunteers to recite the memory verse, or recite it as a group.
3. Invite each woman to share a personal story about discipline (i.e., her parents' disciplining her as a child, a funny story about disciplining her own children, etc.). As each woman shares, reflect on how her story might help illustrate the discussion later in the study.

Discussion

1. **Everyday Woman**—Ask if anyone has found, like Charlene, that her past sin has allowed her to teach or encourage others. Invite the women to share examples while you monitor the time.
2. **Eternal Wisdom**—Discuss questions 3 through 5. Read aloud Hebrews 12:1-11, and then discuss questions 6, 8 and 10. Briefly explain the correlation between pruning and disciplining; then share the fruits of discipline found in questions 11 through 13.
3. **Enduring Hope**—Review the principles of physical muscle growth, and then ask volunteers to share their answers to question 14.
4. **Everyday Life**—Form groups of two or three women each. Have each woman share her answers to questions 15 and 17.
5. **Close in Prayer**—While still in small groups, allow the women time to pray for one another, thanking God for His discipline and asking Him to help them learn their lessons the first time. Have them trade Prayer Request Forms, or index cards, before leaving.

After the Meeting

1. **Evaluate.**
2. **Encourage.**
3. **Equip.**
4. **Pray.**

SESSION EIGHT—
A REASON TO DANCE:
The Character of a Healed Heart

Before the Meeting

1. Make the usual preparations as listed on pages 86-87.

Ice Breakers

1. Distribute the Prayer Request Forms, or index cards, and then remind

the women to write down their names, even if they don't have specific requests this week.

2. Invite volunteers to recite all of the memory verses they have learned during this study. If possible, have someone share how memorizing Scripture has helped her heart heal.

3. Invite volunteers to share ways that they have grown through the course of this study. Allow ample time for this activity, as the main goal of today's session is to reflect on the ways each woman has grown.

Discussion

1. **Everyday Woman**—Discuss the principle of contrasts and ask each women to give an example of a contrast. Or invite discussion on question 1.

2. **Eternal Wisdom**—Read aloud 1 Peter 1:3-7; then discuss questions 2 through 5. Invite volunteers to share ways in which they have experienced freedom in the past eight weeks; then read Galatians 5:1 and discuss why we are the only ones who can put ourselves back into bondage (question 9). Invite volunteers to share the verse they selected in response to question 10 and to explain why they selected it. Discuss questions 11 and 12 if time allows.

3. **Enduring Hope**—Discuss questions 13 and 14, or invite volunteers to describe what they are looking forward to when they get to heaven.

4. **Everyday Life**—Briefly review the text in this section; then invite the women to share how they have been encouraged or sharpened by the stories and experiences other women in the group have shared over the course of the study.

5. **Close in Prayer**—As a group, thank God for the healing He has brought and will continue to bring to their souls. Spend the remaining time worshiping God for who He is through prayer and song.

After the Meeting

1. **Evaluate.**
2. **Encourage.**
3. **Equip.**
4. **Pray.**

We've Combined the Best of Women's Ministry for One Comprehensive Experience!

These resources provide a multitude of ideas for giving women the much-desired opportunity to get together and share different life experiences— joys and sorrows—to build deep, Christ-centered relationships.

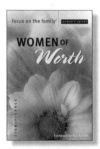

Women of Worth
Bible Study

Women often define themselves by what others expect of them. Many feel they come up short when they try to have it all—beauty, family, career, success. This study helps women find their true identity and purpose through their relationship with Christ. Includes topics such as defining worth, body image, femininity, sexuality and relationships.
ISBN 08307.33361

Healing the Heart
Bible Study

This study helps women experience emotional and spiritual healing by understanding the hurts and pain in their lives and finding restoration through Christ. Topics include recognizing the effects of sin, mending your thoughts, forgiveness and letting go of the past.
ISBN 08307.33620

Balanced Living
Bible Study

When women strive to do it all, they end up feeling stressed out, fatigued and disconnected from God. This study gives women the tools to balance the various demands on their time while maintaining an intimate relationship with God. Topics include why women overextend themselves, separating the important from the urgent and managing the pressures of life.
ISBN 08307.33639

The Blessings of Friendships
Bible Study

In today's fast-paced, busy world it's difficult for women to establish and maintain strong, healthy relationships. In this study, women will explore the nature of relationships and Christ's model for them. Some of the topics covered include forgiveness, being honest and vulnerable, the fine art of listening, receiving correction and the blessings of community.
ISBN 08307.33647

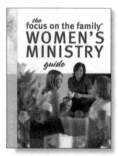

The Focus on the Family
Women's Ministry Guide

This comprehensive guide gives leaders everything they need to set up and run an effective ministry for women of all ages and life situations.
ISBN 08307.33388

Crafts and Activities for
Women's Ministry

This book is packed with ideas for adding fun and creativity to women's ministry meetings and special events. Includes reproducible craft patterns, activities and more!
ISBN 08307.33671

STRENGTHEN MARRIAGES.
STRENGTHEN YOUR CHURCH.

Here's Everything You Need for a Dynamic Marriage Ministry!

Group Starter Kit includes

- Nine Bible Studies: *The Masterpiece Marriage, The Passionate Marriage, The Fighting Marriage, The Model Marriage, The Surprising Marriage, The Giving Marriage, The Covenant Marriage, The Abundant Marriage* and *The Blended Marriage*
- *The Focus on the Family Marriage Ministry Guide*
- *An Introduction to the Focus on the Family Marriage Series* video

Focus on the Family®
Marriage Series
Group Starter Kit
Kit Box
Bible Study/Marriage
ISBN 08307.32365

The overall health of your church is directly linked to the health of its marriages. And in light of today's volatile pressures and changing lifestyles, your commitment to nurture and strengthen marriages needs tangible, practical help. Now **Focus on the Family— the acknowledged leader in Christian marriage and family resources**—gives churches a comprehensive group study series dedicated to enriching marriages. Strengthen marriages and strengthen your church with **The Focus on the Family Marriage Series.**

The Focus on the Family Women's Series
is available where Christian books are sold.

Gospel Light